My Best Togs
(Everyday sayings: their origins and spiritual applications)

My Best Togs

(Everyday sayings: their origins and spiritual applications)

'Who are these people dressed in white robes, and where do they come from?' (Revelation 7:13)

by
James Northey

International Headquarters of The Salvation Army
101 Queen Victoria Street, London EC4P 4EP

Copyright © 1985 The General of The Salvation Army
First published 1985
ISBN 0 85412 465 9

MAJOR JAMES NORTHEY
was commissioned as a Salvation Army officer in 1948. He served
as a corps officer for 14½ years and with The Salvation Army
Assurance Society for nine years. He was appointed to the Literary
Department, International Headquarters, in 1971 and became
Assistant Literary Secretary in 1978. The major is author of *I'll go
to China, Outreach* and *My Father's House.*

Art work by Jim Moss

Printed in Great Britain by
The Campfield Press, St Albans

CONTENTS

Reading:
Page

Foreword

1 I'll put on my best togs 1
2 It was a red-letter day 4
3 You'll have to take pot luck 6
4 He's not worth his salt 9
5 He'll have to come up to scratch 11
6 She's from a posh family 13
7 She always paid on the nail 15
8 It's not worth the candle. 18
9 Your name is Mudd 21
10 I'm so tired I could sleep on a clothes line .. 24
11 They gave her the cold shoulder 27
12 Don't let the cat out of the bag 30
13 A baker's dozen 33
14 He's a big wig 36
15 They were caught napping 39
16 She took umbrage 42
17 She saved her bacon 46
18 She was a grass widow 49
19 They've settled a bargain 52
20 It's been earmarked for you 55
21 He's often in the limelight 58
22 Let me kiss the place and make it better .. 62
23 He let himself go to pot 64
24 I was roped in to help 67
25 He had a busman's holiday 71
26 She served us Adam's ale 74

Foreword

THE initial reason for writing this book was to meet a need expressed by some leaders of over-60 clubs in The Salvation Army for spiritual messages to be given during their weekly meeting. I have endeavoured to use simple, everyday English bearing in mind the readings are meant to be read in public.

To facilitate public reading by those who are not particularly adept in this art, I have used what could be regarded as more-than-necessary punctuation, and to make things easier on the reader's eyes the size of printer's type is bigger than usual. The references for Scripture quotations (which are from the *Good News Bible,* unless otherwise stated)* are placed as footnotes to avoid their being needlessly mentioned during the reading, but it is hoped that the reader will familiarise himself/herself with the context in which quotes are found.

It is important that the reader should practise reading aloud in private and he/she should recognise that reading in public is effective only if there is variation in pace, tone, volume and emphasis, and pauses in appropriate places will add to the dramatic effect.

Since possibly many listeners will have only a limited knowledge of the Scriptures, generally I have referred to the chosen portions by writing, 'In the Bible we read' or 'The Bible says', instead of, for example, 'The writer to the Hebrews says'.

I think readers will find that most of the readings are aimed at the unconverted. Although primarily written for over-60 club meetings, I have been encouraged to offer them also for possible use at home league meetings, meetings in old people's homes, hospitals and even in prisons. And perhaps they could be adapted for use during beach meetings held in seaside resorts.

A further suggestion is that perhaps members of a carefully-chosen cast with imagination could mime what is being read. This might prove suitable as an item for a festival or rally. If the readings can be used, in whatever chosen way, to reach the hearts of the hearers with their simple gospel message, that will be reward enough for the author.

J.N.

*Scripture quotations, unless otherwise stated, from the *Good News Bible*. © American Bible Society 1976, published by the Bible Societies/ Collins. Used by permission.

Abbreviations used for other Bible versions: *AV,* Authorised Version; *NEB,* New English Bible; *LB,* The Living Bible; *JBP,* J. B. Phillips.

1
I'll put on my best togs

WHEN a woman is invited to a wedding, or perhaps to meet the Queen, her first thought is, 'What shall I wear?' She will want to look her best. If she is married, her husband might have to write out a cheque to cover the cost of her new outfit, including an eye-catching hat! And, of course, being the loving husband that he is, he gladly obliges!

When the great day arrives, and her partner waits to accompany her to the exciting event, his patience is sorely tried as he waits and waits for her to put on her new, best togs! (Have you heard the story of the man who wrote a book in the odd minutes he had to spend waiting for his wife to get ready to go out with him?)

Our slang word 'togs' comes from the Roman word 'toga' and has been part of the English language for about 300 years. A toga was a loose, flowing outer garment worn by ancient Roman citizens. When a Roman boy reached the age of 14, he was eligible to wear a plain white toga as a sign of his manhood.

In the story of the crucifixion of Jesus there's an interesting incident in which Roman soldiers, having shared out his clothing, obviously recognised the beauty of Christ's seamless robe and drew lots to decide who among them should become the owner. Here's the actual account: they 'took the robe, which was made of one piece of woven cloth without any seams in it. The soldiers said to one another, "Let's not tear it; let's throw dice to see who will get it"'.[1] We may imagine a proud, off-duty Roman soldier wearing that robe and perhaps thinking of it as his best togs. But we can be sure that wearing our Lord's beautiful coat didn't make him like Jesus in spirit or in character.

The Bible speaks about an enormous crowd of people from every race dressed in white robes standing before the throne of God.[2] In symbolic language God's word then says about them, 'They have washed their robes and made them white with the blood of the Lamb'.[3] In other words, their hearts had been cleansed from all sin. They had asked for, and received, the forgiveness of God for their sins, a priceless gift made possible to everybody by the sacrificial offering of Jesus on the cross.

In another book of the Bible we find words addressed to women which emphasise that outward beauty aids 'such as the way you do your hair, or the jewellery you put on, or the dresses you wear',[4] can't go deep enough to produce real beauty. (After all, what is attractive about a woman who is beautifully dressed if she's always grumbling?) The Bible goes on to say, 'your beauty should consist of your true inner self, the ageless beauty of a gentle and quiet spirit, which is of the greatest value in God's sight'.[5]

Let us, of course, continue to keep ourselves outwardly attractive and enjoy the satisfaction that comes when occasionally somebody expresses admiration of the clothes we wear or simply gives an approving glance. It's good for our morale. But when we wear the inner white robe of a cleansed and forgiven-by-God life; and when we show a loving, gracious spirit, we are dressed in the timeless, beautiful fashion created according to our heavenly Father's design. And we know the joy of his eye of approval. We are, then, really wearing our best togs!

---

1 John 19:23b, 24a

2 See Revelation 7:9-17

3 Revelation 7:14b

4 1 Peter 3:3

5 1 Peter 3:4

2
It was a red-letter day

WE all remember red-letter days, days on which we had unforgettable, joyful experiences. The day we married, for example, or the day we left school to take up our first job. A true story is told of a housewife who walked backwards when she set off for the shops on 27.9.1972. It was oddly enough a red-letter day for her because the date reads the same backwards—2-7-9-1-9-7-2—and so she held her own celebration to mark it. One wonders whether she repeated her strange act on 28.9.1982, another date which forms a numerical palindrome (from the Greek, *palindromos,* meaning running back again).

The phrase 'red-letter day' stems from the time when Saints' Days, on which special festivities were held, were marked on our calendars in red letters. There was, for instance, St David's Day: 1 March; St Patrick's Day: 17 March; St George's Day: 23 April; and St Andrew's Day: 30 November.

There was a time when all calendars in Christian Britain showed Sundays in red letters as well, but sadly few publishers keep up this tradition. In the Bible we read, 'Observe the Sabbath and keep it holy. You have six days in which to do your work, but the seventh day is a day of rest dedicated to me. On that day no one is to work. . . .'[1]

Orthodox Jews keep this commandment of God by not working on Saturday, and some go to such lengths in observing their Sabbath that they will not even switch on an electric light. For the Christian, the Sabbath is Sunday, or the Lord's Day. The change was made many centuries ago to commemorate the day on which Jesus rose from the dead—a red-letter day indeed!

4

The man or woman whose heart has been deeply stirred by what our Lord did for him or her by dying on the cross and then defeating death itself, is glad of the gift of Sunday, the day set apart to worship God and to remember with gratitude his love as portrayed in Christ; to sing, speak and pray in praise to God for the glorious fact that Jesus is alive for evermore.

The word 'holiday' was formerly 'holy day'. Apart from the Lord's Day being a holy day on which we worship, it's a holiday on which we cut ourselves off from the routine of work at factory, office or shop and even in the home we do only the necessary tasks.

Some people don't think it's wrong to participate in sports on Sunday, but anything which takes the place of the worship of God is breaking this command about the Sabbath. Eric Liddell was a competitor in the 1924 Olympics. He was also a devout Christian and held a deep conviction concerning the purpose of the Lord's Day. He refused to run in the heats for the 100 metres race held on Sunday. Later he participated in the 400 metres, over which distance his chances weren't good, and won a gold medal!

There's at least a two-fold benefit in obeying God's command to observe the Sabbath or Lord's Day. It brings renewed strength to soul and to body and we return to our daily work with fresh zeal. And we may be sure that God honours those who honour him and his commands.

---

1 Exodus 20:8-10*a*

3
You'll have to take pot luck

HOW many of us remember the open fireplace with its blazing, welcoming fire on a cold day; with its black, polished ironwork and shining, deep brass fender and burnished side-oven door knob? In the centre, on a swivelling, iron stand suspended over the fire, stood a large iron kettle holding water which was always on the boil, the steam gently escaping up the chimney from the spout. Perhaps on the burning coals was a large cooking pot containing whatever was to be the main meal that day.

To 'take pot luck' originates from those days.

Unexpected visitors would be warmly welcomed and invited to share a meal, but with the gentle caution that no special preparation could be made. They would have to share with the family whatever happened to be in the pot on the fire.

The Bible tells us to 'remember to welcome strangers in your homes' for 'there were some who did that and welcomed angels without knowing it'.[1] Have you read the captivating story about Jesus who, after he had risen from the dead, appeared to two of his disciples on the Emmaus Road? They thought he was a stranger in that district. They were sad because Jesus had died, and the sorrow showed on their faces. When they reached home and still didn't recognise their Master, they invited him to have bed and breakfast. And it was free. There's no mention of a charge!

Telling this fascinating story, the New Testament records the actual words of that kind invitation. They were, ' "Stay with us; the day is almost over and it is getting dark".' And then the saga continues: 'So he went in to stay with them. He sat down to eat with them, took the bread, and said the blessing; then he broke the bread and gave it to them. Then their eyes were opened and they recognised him, but he disappeared from their sight. They said to each other, "Wasn't it like a fire burning in us when he talked to us on the road and explained the Scriptures to us?" '[2]

Nowadays we often hear of unwelcome strangers forcing their way into the homes of the elderly. It might be unwise to open our doors to callers we don't recognise or expect. But this shouldn't make us feel inhospitable. Provided we keep and develop the spirit of welcome for all genuine visitors, and even if we can offer them only a cup of tea, that would be pleasing to God.

Salvationists sometimes sing:

> *Once I heard a sound at my heart's dark door*
> *And was roused from the slumber of sin;*
> *It was Jesus knocked, He had knocked before,*
> *Now I said: Blessed Master, come in!*

If a welcome into your home and heart is extended to the Lord Jesus Christ, who was gladly received into that Emmaus home, this guest will give you the biggest blessing of your life. And like the two disciples in the story, your depression and discouragement, a result of the disappointing way things may have turned out for you, will disappear in an instant and you'll face the future, despite the trials it might hold, with divine strength and eternal hope.

---

1 Hebrews 13:2   2 Luke 24:29-32

4
He's not worth his salt

SOME people receive wages for work done. Others are given a salary. But when it comes down to the economic facts of life, they both mean the same—money. The word 'salary' derives from a Latin word 'salarium', meaning 'salt money', a payment made to Roman soldiers to buy salt. When someone is said to be not worth his salt it means that he doesn't deserve the payment he's received for the poor job done, or doesn't merit the privilege given to him.

The Bible exhorts us, 'Work hard at whatever you do'.[1] It also says, 'The workman is worth his keep!'[2] That, of course, refers to a good workman. The great Apostle Paul urged his young assistant, Timothy, to 'concentrate on winning God's approval, on being a workman with nothing to be ashamed of'.[3]

When I was in charge of Jarrow-on-Tyne Salvation Army Corps, one of the salvationists invited me to watch the launching of a new ship on which he had worked as a sign-writer. As the giant hull slid gracefully into the river, stern first, this friend, who was standing by me, pointed to the name of the vessel on the bow, *Olynthus,* and told me with obvious and legitimate pride that he painted it. Here was a man proud of a job well done and he deserved his wages. He was worth his salt.

We live in an age in which so many people have little interest in their work and the result is shoddy workmanship. Wouldn't it be wise to have an occasional national campaign with the slogan, *Do Your Best!*? Everybody in offices, shops, factories, and at school, college and home seeking to produce the best they are capable of and so helping to regain our national pride and reputation for work well done. And, I think, this would give a much-needed boost to our national economy and result in less unemployment and a consequent higher standard of living for many more people.

Even in retirement some people find tasks and hobbies to which they conscientiously apply heart, mind and muscle, since they recognise that the same application which brought satisfaction in a job well done in wage-earning years, must continue in life's evening years. It's good for the mind and spirit of the worker. It helps to maintain a zest for living. Indeed, it brings its own reward, one which money can't buy. And it pleases God, as well.

---

1 Ecclesiastes 9:10*a*   2 Matthew 10:10*b*, *JBP*
3 2 Timothy 2:15, *JBP*

5
He'll have to come up to scratch

IN the days when bare fists were used in boxing matches, each participant had to begin the fight with his left foot on a line scratched on the ground between them. The line at the start of a race is also called the scratch. It would be said of an athlete who neglected his training programme that he would never come up to scratch. This meant that he wouldn't be fit enough to appear at the starting line of an important race.

We might have great expectations of somebody as a pianist or tennis player, for example, but as time passes, having noticed their waning spirit of determination, we are compelled to say, 'He'll have to put in a lot of hard study and practice before he comes up to scratch'.

A well-known hymn likens the Christian life to a race. It exhorts us to:

> Run the straight race through God's good grace,
> Lift up thine eyes and seek his face;
> Life with its way before us lies,
> Christ is the path, and Christ the prize.

And in the Bible we can find advice which says, 'Since we have such a huge crowd of men of faith watching us from the grandstands, let us strip off anything that slows us down or holds us back, and especially those sins that wrap themselves so tightly around our feet and trip us up; and let us run with patience the particular race that God has set before us. Keep your eyes on Jesus, our leader and instructor.'[1]

And to come up to scratch, spiritually speaking, so that we win the prize of eternal life, we must act upon that advice and follow Jesus and obey his instructions and so maintain our spiritual fitness for the Christian race.

In another book of the Bible we read, 'Surely you know that many runners take part in a race, but only one of them wins the prize. Run, then, in such a way as to win the prize. Every athlete in training submits to strict discipline, in order to be crowned with a wreath that will not last; but we do it for one that will last for ever. That is why I run straight for the finishing-line . . .'[2] And by the 'finishing-line' the writer meant reaching Heaven!

---

1 Hebrews 12:1, 2a, *LB*   2 1 Corinthians 9:24-26a

6
She's from a posh family

WHEN we say, 'that's posh' we mean it's superior. Using the same slang phrase in relation to a person or people, usually we are referring to them as belonging to a wealthy family. To discover how the word 'posh' was coined it has been said that we have to go back to the days before flying when wealthy people with financial interests in India would journey to that land, some possibly to escape the rigours of the British winter, by the old P & O shipping line. To avoid the discomfort of the hot sun on the starboard *(right)* side when the ship turned east into the Mediterranean and later steamed across the Indian Ocean, these people booked expensive cabins on the port *(left)* side. When they arranged to sail back to the United Kingdom, the booking of berths was for the starboard side for the same reason, the hot sun now concentrating its rays on the port side.

So it was *P*ort (side) *O*ut (to the east) and *S*tarboard (side) *H*ome (to UK). Since only rich people could afford the privilege, that's how they became known as POSH folk.

A lot of people envy the rich and imagine if they became wealthy all their problems would be solved. They would retire, buy a large detached house standing in its own grounds, go on world cruises and generally 'live it up'. It would, they think, be heaven on earth.

Money left by a relative in his will is sometimes the cause of a family row. The greater the amount of money the greater the row. The degree of anger in any one member of the family is decided or fixed by what attitude he has already adopted toward material things. If he places little value on money, being content to pay his way and enjoy a simple life-style, he won't be over-concerned about receiving what others might call his fair share of his father's estate. On the other hand the man who loves and lives for money will fight hard and even angrily to obtain every penny he feels is due to him and more.

A man listening to our Lord Jesus was probably of the latter kind. Let us read what the Bible says: 'A man in the crowd said to Jesus, "Teacher, tell my brother to divide with me the property our father left us." Jesus answered him, "My friend, who gave me the right to judge or to divide the property between you two?" And he went on to say to them all, "Watch out and guard yourselves from every kind of greed; because a person's true life is not made up of the things he owns, no matter how rich he may be"'.[1]

Observation of people confirms the truth of our Lord's words. Whilst some rich people give generously to alleviate the sufferings of the world's poor, others are among the most unhappy despite their great material wealth.

Although there's no virtue in poverty and good men and women have worked hard, and still work hard, to eliminate it, some of the poorest people are among the happiest people in the world, because they've discovered and enjoy the spiritual riches of Christ.

---

1 Luke 12:13-15

7

She always paid
on the nail

MOST of us know that to 'pay on the nail' means to pay our debts in full and without delay, provided, of course, we are satisfied the correct amount has been charged. But although we are familiar with the meaning of this saying, many of us are puzzled about its origin.

To find the solution we must journey back in time to the Middle Ages, at least 400 years ago. In some of the open markets of those days, we should see official 'payment counters'. They were waist-high, flat-topped pillars knows as 'nails'. One of these 'nails', we are told, can still be seen in Bristol.

How many of us remember the time when working-class mothers with large families to feed and clothe had to keep a strict check on the way they spent their meagre amount of weekly housekeeping money? That was in the days when state social security 'hand outs' were non-existent. To cover the cost of items such as gas and coal; to ensure there was money to pay the rent and 1d or even ½d weekly premiums on life assurance policies, they would place in different tins the various amounts due to be 'paid on the nail' when the various collectors called at their humble homes. What was left would be used to buy food, sufficient to provide only a frugal diet, and other basic necessities such as clothing. The latter was affordable only rarely. What experts some of these mothers became in the art of patching, darning and sewing. 'Make do and mend' was their slogan because they had no other choice. Many of these courageous women had little or no education and probably had never heard of the word 'economics' but sheer necessity made them fine economists.

The question of payment of taxes is raised several times in the Bible. There is an instance when a group of our Lord's opponents tried to trap him in his own words. Here is the Bible account of this incident which took place when the Romans occupied Palestine and decreed that its inhabitants had to pay certain taxes to them: '"Give us your ruling on this: are we or are we not permitted to pay taxes to the Roman Emperor?" Jesus was aware of their malicious intention and said to them, "You hypocrites! Why are you trying to catch me out? Show me the money in which the tax is paid." They handed him a silver piece. Jesus asked, "Whose head is this, and whose inscription?" "Caesar's", they replied. He said to them, "Then pay Caesar what is due to Caesar, and pay God what is due to God".'[1]

Let us observe here that Jesus clearly says we have a two-fold duty. We must pay our taxes and, of course, all our bills. And he implies we must respect the law of the land; we must give honour to those in authority over us at every level. All these are included in our Lord's command, 'Pay Caesar what is due to Caesar'. But he also said, 'Pay God what is due to God'.

Relatively few people seek to dodge paying their taxes. And most of us pay all our bills 'on the nail'. In fact we are rightly proud of our good reputation in this matter. But how many of us are still piling up a great debt by not paying to God what we owe him?

If you think that Jesus was talking about paying or giving money to help to maintain and extend the work of Christian missions in, say, the Third World—for example, feeding the starving, healing the sick, housing the homeless and preaching the Christian message—you'll be partly correct, since we have a responsibility in that direction.

But let us look more closely at Christ's reply to his crafty questioners. Before saying they had to pay their debts to Caesar, he asked them whose head or image was on the silver coin he held in his hand. It was Caesar's, they replied.

If I asked anybody living in Britain to show me the image of Queen Elizabeth II, this would be easy to do because her head is on every coin and currency note in their purse.

It seems to me that Jesus might well have been thinking of the image of God with which every human being is born, as the Bible tells us. In the first book of the Bible we read that God said, 'Let us make man in our image, after our likeness'.[2] It is common practice to mark what belongs to us with our name or some other identifying mark. Apart from the fact that God's intention was—and still is—that we should bear his likeness in character, can we see that being created in his image identifies us as belonging to him? This suggests that when Jesus told his questioners to pay God what is due to God, the whole of our being should be given to God for his glory and to be used in his service.

The shape of the heart is regarded as the symbol of love but, of course, when the Christian speaks of having given his heart to God he means, not the organ that pumps blood around his body, but his will or the very heart of his personality from which flows all his thoughts, words, desires and actions. Each practising Christian came to the point of commitment of his heart to God when he realised something of the great love shown to all mankind in the giving of his Son Jesus to die for everybody's sin. It was this deeply-moving revelation of our heavenly Father's loving heart that caused Isaac Watts, the hymn-writer, to pray:

Dear Saviour I can ne'er repay
The debt of love I owe!
Here, Lord, I give myself away;
'Tis all that I can do.

Have you made this prayer, your prayer?

---

1 Matthew 22:17-21, *NEB*   2 Genesis 1:26, *AV*

8
It's not worth the candle

BEFORE the days when lighting by gas and electricity came into being, theatres were lit by candles which were held by boys. Whether the theatre-goers had to pay for the candles in addition to their admission fee isn't clear. It would seem, however, that this was so, since if the acting was poor the patrons would say it wasn't worth the candle, and that's how this saying became part of the English language.

It's now almost 2,000 years since Jesus came on to the stage of human life and took the star or leading role. He was indeed the brightest star by far that this world had ever seen or will ever see. He himself said, 'I am the bright morning star'.[1]

His performance on the world stage, though, didn't please the religious leaders of his day. They should have been the first to applaud the appearance of this glorious, shining light. In fact they were so displeased that their disapproval turned to hate. The Bible tells the story of this great star and the reaction of his own race: 'God sent his messenger, a man named John, who came to tell people about the light, so that all should hear the message and believe. He himself was not the light; he came to tell about the light. This was the real light—the light that comes into the world and shines on all mankind. The Word was in the world, and though God made the world through him, yet the world did not recognise him. He came to his own country, but his own people did not receive him. Some, however, did receive him and believed in him; so he gave them the right to become God's children.'[2]

So we see that on the opening night when Jesus came on stage it seemed that he wouldn't have a successful run. It appeared at first that his performance would be a flop. Events increasingly pointed that way because eventually he was arrested, taken to court, tried and found guilty on false charges. The death sentence was passed on him and he had to endure the shame and agony of crucifixion, a form of execution reserved for the worst of criminals. What is more he had to bear the humiliation of being crucified in public, in full view of hundreds, possibly thousands, of onlookers. His role as a star had ended; his light extinguished, or so his enemies thought. But the Bible says about this Light that 'the darkness has never put it out'.[3]

Three days later that great Light broke out of a tomb and it has continued to shine ever since bringing enlightenment and hope to millions who have gladly accepted him, 'the light of the world',[4] as their director

19

in the everyday performance of Christlike living. They testify with joy in their hearts that Christ is the greatest star to have ever appeared on the human stage. They feel highly privileged to co-star with Jesus. They invite everybody to join their great supporting cast; to take on the role of a Christian. And they say it's worth every bit of the cost of the candle, and much more besides!

---

1 Revelation 22:16*b*   2 John 1:6-12
3 John 1:5*b*   4 John 8:12*a*

9
Your name is Mudd

UNLESS there's a reason to feel otherwise, everybody's proud of his or her family name. Doctor Samuel Mudd was probably no exception, but sadly this man's name is directly linked with the saying, 'your name is Mudd'. This is how it happened. When President Abraham Lincoln of the United States of America was assassinated in 1865, the man responsible for this terrible deed fractured a leg while making his escape. Managing to reach the isolation of the countryside, the assassin obtained medical attention from the doctor who was unaware of the awful crime committed by his new patient. The next day, news of the president's tragic death reached him and he immediately suspected the stranger with a broken leg. As a dutiful citizen, Doctor Mudd at once reported his suspicion to the police, but soon afterwards he himself was arrested, tried and sentenced to life imprisonment as a conspirator. He was not only unjustly imprisoned, his name has ever since been unfairly used as a description of anybody accused, truly or falsely, of some bad deed, and even in a semi-serious way when some remark has unintentionally caused offence.

Being wrongly accused of evil words or act, or to have one's name unfairly linked with them, or to be misunderstood or misrepresented, is one of the hardest things to bear. This is especially difficult if we are practising Christians, and if what has happened causes people to think less about our Christianity. But our Lord, who fully understands from personal, bitter experience what it's like to be treated wrongly, said to his disciples, 'Happy are those who are persecuted because they do what God requires; the Kingdom of heaven belongs to them! Happy are you when people insult you and persecute you and tell all kinds of evil lies against you because you are my followers. Be happy and glad, for a great reward is kept for you in heaven'.[1]

When we are treated unjustly, as was the unfortunate Dr Mudd, it usually makes us the opposite of being happy. So whatever did Jesus mean when he said his followers should be happy when they are insulted? Let us imagine we are going on a hazardous journey across the world. It will include sailing on storm-tossed seas, struggling through swampy, crocodile-infested country and battling with venomous snakes and other dangerous, wild creatures. Such experiences would normally fill us with great fear, but on this journey we know that we shall safely reach our destination because of an awareness of the guardianship of a loving, all-powerful, although invisible, power. Having advance knowledge about our safe-landing, isn't it true to say that some might even enjoy being tossed about in a boat by mountainous waves, or being attacked by vicious wild animals? Knowing that our safety is assured would certainly bring peace instead of fear, and some of us might even find that kind of life exciting. The great saint Paul, it seems, discovered this secret for he declared, 'I can even enjoy weaknesses, suffering, privations, persecutions and difficulties for Christ's sake'.[2] Salvationists sometimes sing:

> Following Jesus, ever day by day,
> Nothing can harm me while he leads the way. . . .

Does all this help us to see what Jesus meant when he said, 'Happy are you when people insult you and persecute you and tell all kinds of evil lies against you because you are my followers'?[3]

Our Lord doesn't, of course, promise his people protection from physical harm, although many of them can testify to that. In fact others have been killed because they followed him. But there's a part of a Christian, the eternal part, which can't be harmed by evil. It is the soul. We so readily think of our real life only in terms of the 70 or so years we live in the body.

But Jesus views our life in the light of eternity. It is our eternal well-being that is his prime concern. Warning his disciples of the possible physical dangers of being his followers, Christ told them, 'Never be afraid of those who can kill the body but are powerless to kill the soul!'[4]

The person who truly follows Jesus, despite any form of suffering it entails, can be happy because our Lord has assured him that his real, eternal self is beyond the reach of evil. How? Because he is in the care of our all-powerful, loving heavenly Father.

---

1 Matthew 5:10-12

2 2 Corinthians 12:10, *JBP*

3 Matthew 5:11

4 Matthew 10:28, *JBP*

10
I'm so tired I could sleep on a clothes line

HAVE you heard of 'the two-penny rope'? If you had been a down-and-out man in, say, London in the 19th century, this rope would have been your 'bed'! These poor men, who couldn't afford even the price of the cheapest bed in common lodging houses, were provided with a bench on which they sat during the long hours of the night. In front of them a clothes line was tightly stretched. For this provision they presumably paid tuppence each, hence the rope's name. Unable to lie down they were simply glad to lean their weary bodies against the rope. But early in the morning they were

rudely awakened from their fitful slumbers when the landlord cut the rope!

In an age when many people have difficulty falling asleep when they retire for the night, and many millions of sleeping pills are prescribed by doctors, sleep is a topical subject. Research and experimentation is being conducted into the problems of insomnia, sleeplessness, and its opposite malady, narcolepsy, a condition suffered by people who have sudden fits of sleepiness, even while working, and are therefore a possible danger to themselves and others.

Some people need at least eight hours sleep in 24; others can manage on four or five. One man claimed that since he was injured in an accident many months earlier he had been unable to sleep at all.

While travelling home on a train returning from the city early one evening, I noticed a middle-aged man sitting next to me was reading a book entitled, *How to sleep better.* He had reached the second page of chapter two. After turning my eyes in another direction for a few minutes, my gaze casually returned to the book and its reader. I was amused to find that he was dozing! He was a picture of peace! Was the book about sleeping better having instant effect? Or was he simply bored by what he read? More likely the poor man was simply catching up with sleep lost during the previous night, and nights before that!

For many people life has become burdensome and, being so tired of trying to cope, some try to forget their troubles in, say, drugs or drink. But such things bring them only temporary and false relief. Their deep-seated problem remains. In some cases their plight is the result of their own sin. Others are languishing through no fault of their own. But for all of them the Lord Jesus Christ has a comforting word. It's also a heart-warming, hope-giving invitation, and it's been recorded in the Bible as a standing invitation for every genera-tion. Here is how it reads, 'Come to me, all of you who are tired from carrying heavy loads, and I will give you rest. Take my yoke and put it on you, and learn from me, because I am gentle and humble in spirit; and you will find rest. For the yoke I will give you is easy, and the load I will put on you is light.'[1]

---

1 Matthew 11:28-30

11

They gave her the cold shoulder

IT was probably in Victorian times, or even earlier, that this saying became part of the English language. When an unexpected, unwanted visitor arrived, gentle hints were dropped by the host to encourage an early departure and to discourage similar calls in future. To save face, though, the hostess felt obliged to provide a meal for the unwelcome guest but would serve only what required the minimum of preparation, the cold remains of the shoulder of meat left over from the previous evening's family dinner. From this we learn the origin of the saying 'they gave her the cold shoulder'.

There's a story in the Bible[1] about a man who became angry when he heard that his younger brother had returned home after a long absence. This lad was the black sheep of the family and had caused a lot of worry for his dad, whose money he'd been wasting in a far off country. Throughout those years his elder brother had answered his rich father's every beck and call as he slaved on the family farm. Perhaps there were times when he felt the need of the extra help his brother could have given.

One day as he trudged home after another hard, tiring day on the land he was astonished to hear music and see people dancing as he approached the house. He called a servant to ask what was going on. The reply he received was like the proverbial last straw! Angrily he asked himself, 'Has my dad really put on a lavish dinner-party to celebrate the return of this ne'er-do-well son of his? He's never arranged a party to show gratitude for my long and loyal service'. He continued, 'And why didn't

27

he send a servant into the field where I was working to at least warn me about what was happening at home? Was it because he knew my attitude to his prodigal son, and that I wouldn't want to share in the welcome-home party? In any case I wouldn't want to humiliate myself by being seen in my dusty working clothes when the revellers were in their Sunday best, would I? And wouldn't I have to explain to the guests why I wasn't joining in the merrymaking?'

With these questions racing through his mind it isn't surprising to learn that he refused to enter the house. And even when his father finally came out to plead with him, he remained adamant about not going inside.

To be fair to the father, though, it must be said that he told the elder son that everything he owned belonged to him. Having learned this, we can easily imagine that had the father died before the younger son's return and the elder brother had taken possession of the family home, the younger lad would indeed have received the cold shoulder instead of the fatted calf his father killed and roasted to celebrate his return. In fact he would have been treated so coldly that he would have been frozen out of the house!

In this story, which is one of the best-known parables told by Jesus Christ, we see two contrasting emotions towards a wayward son and brother who sincerely wanted to make amends for his wrong doing and to be reconciled. The first is anger stemming from hate; the other is joy springing from the loving heart of the father.

One of the truths Jesus is illustrating in this parable is that our Father in Heaven welcomes the person who truly admits he has sinned and longs for pardon and reconciliation with him. We also learn that the self-righteousness of the elder brother, whose loyalty to his father couldn't be faulted, was however a greater sin. It is the sin many of us commit and it often makes impossible any reconciliation between people.

In fact, unless our hearts are motivated by the love of God we are more likely to give the cold shoulder to those who have offended us; but the way to reconciliation and to friendship between people is to show the warmth of forgiveness and offer a sincere welcome. After all who among us hasn't at some time offended others? And don't most of us feel remorse and sadness because of our unkind words or deeds and long to be forgiven and reconciled and to enjoy again the warmth of true friendship?

---

1 Luke 15:11-32

12
Don't let the cat out of the bag

THIS saying stems from a dishonest practice related to the time when piglets were taken to market in a bag. Among the piglets would be one or two surplus farm cats which, it was hoped, would be passed off to unwary buyers. But because cats don't like being kept in confinement, at the first chance of freedom they make their lightning escape. Sometimes the unscrupulous seller holding the mouth of the bag of piglets would unconsciously and momentarily release his grip and a cat would leap out. Everybody watching the sale would instantly know about his secret dishonesty.

Of course, the saying has become one to describe the action of anybody giving away, unwittingly or deliberately, any kind of secret. For instance, when my first grandson was only two years old, he secretly told me that his mother had made me a birthday cake! He let the cat out of the bag!

I think there's another way we could apply this phrase. Jesus advised us not to tell anybody about the good deeds we do for needy people. Let's read his actual words: 'When you give something to a needy person, do not make a big show of it, as the hypocrites do. . . . But when you help a needy person, do it in such a way that even your closest friend will not know about it. Then it will be a private matter.'[1]

There are two observations we might make about this. We shouldn't boast about what we do for, or give to, somebody in need because should that person hear about it, our boasting could have the effect of making him feel inferior to us. This is probably why some people refuse to accept what they call 'charity'. Giving to the needy should always build up their self-esteem.

Then our giving must always be done in the light of God's giving to us. This is especially so in relation to what we read in the Bible about the great gift to the world, to us individually, of God's Son. It reads: 'For God loved the world so much that he gave his only Son, so that everyone who believes in him may not die but have eternal life'.[2] How paltry our giving is in comparison with what God has given to us in Jesus.

To illustrate, let us imagine a man whose physical health has been bad for many years. He has undergone many tests and received numerous forms of treatment, but his health doesn't improve. One day he hears of someone who can give him a new body, one which can't be infected by disease, a body which will live forever. He joyfully accepts the great offer. The gift becomes his. His new life seems too good to be real. But it is!

Can anybody think that when this man now gives something to a needy person he will make a big show of it? No, for he will have become so grateful and humbled by the priceless gift he has received that anything he gives, even though it might be costly in the eyes of the receiver, will be only a tiny token of the deep gratitude in his heart, and will seem as nothing, and certainly not even worth mentioning. He will have learned to put what he gives, into its right perspective.

Jesus spoke about being born again.[3] When we were born we had a brand-new body. But our Lord wasn't talking about a new physical body but a spiritual rebirth to a life which lasts forever. Those who have received this new spiritual body, or life, marvel at the wonder of it all. Provided that by prayer and meditation on God's word they keep their sense of wonder because of the great gift they've accepted from Christ, they will not 'let the cat out of the bag', by telling everybody of how generous they are to needy people. They are simply glad quietly to show their gratitude by helping and giving to others in the name of Christ!

---

1 Matthew 6:2-4   2 John 3:16
3 See John 3:3

13

A baker's dozen

IN the Middle Ages the weight of bread and rolls was strictly monitored and any baker giving under weight was severely dealt with. We can well understand the anxiety of honest bakers who feared they might accidentally provide a customer with a short supply. In an attempt to avoid this and the consequences, they added a 13th item to each dozen ordered and so came into being our saying 'a baker's dozen'.

In some countries of the world the question, 'Where can we buy bread?' is on the lips of the starving multitudes every day. We in the West never have to ask that question. But that is not completely true since, as recently as 1977, there was a strike in the bread trade in the United Kingdom and we saw long queues outside some bakeries, some people forming the queue early in the morning to make sure of their precious supply.

It might have been called a baking question. It was certainly a burning one at the time of the bread strike, when it must have been on the lips of every housewife in the land. Oddly enough, it was also asked about 2,000 years ago. The question, 'Where can we buy bread . . .?'[1] was, in fact, asked by Jesus and put to his disciples.

Although Jesus knew the answer to his own enquiry, he wanted his followers to become involved in meeting the immediate need of the hungry crowd, and to test their faith in him. The story tells that our Lord himself then miraculously provided the bread.

The next day Jesus surprised some of the people who had eaten some of the bread and had followed him to the other side of the sea, by declaring, 'I am the bread of life'.[2] And when he went on to say, 'If anyone eats this bread, he will live for ever,'³ they were naturally puzzled. No wonder they asked, 'How can this man give us his flesh to eat?'⁴

About 500 years earlier the prophet Ezekiel was given a difficult task. God wanted him to deliver a stern warning to the people of Israel. Having received the scroll containing the message, God then told him to do an odd thing. He had to *eat* the scroll before going off to proclaim God's threat! The message had to become part of the messenger.

From this incident in his life, Ezekiel has left us a vivid account of what he discovered. '"Eat it all," he [God] said. And when I ate it, it tasted sweet as honey.'⁵

Jesus didn't mean, of course, that his hearers had to eat his flesh in the literal sense. But those who desired abundant life must yield their wills to his. The life and spirit of Christ had to permeate every part of the lives of those who wanted to taste the sweetness of God's approval.

Many people have the false notion that doing God's will means being deprived of a full and free life. The seemingly hard words, 'Thy will be done', are associated, in their thinking, only with solemn, sad events. They forget that sunshine is part of God's will for us just as much as rain.

Certainly, as Ezekiel discovered, doing God's will sometimes includes hard tasks which demand great courage. Becoming a Christian and then remaining one is, indeed, a manly (or womanly) business.

But note that Ezekiel had such a pleasant surprise when he found that the scroll containing the message tasted sweet. It could be said that the demand made by God was indeed sour to his taste, and only when he obeyed God did he find how sweet God's will really was. The psalmist in the Old Testament made a similar discovery when he declared, 'How sweet is the taste of your instructions—sweeter even than honey!'.⁶

The testimony of millions of committed Christians is that Christ's call to repent was no easy thing to do. But when they did, they tasted the sweetness of Christ, the bread of life. And his supply of bread is never short. He gives far more than the generous baker's dozen. It is always available; always fresh. It is daily bread.

---

1 See John 6:5

3 John 6:51

5 Ezekiel 3:3, *LB*

2 John 6:48

4 John 6:52

6 Psalm 119:103

14
He's a big wig

THIS saying dates from the time when most men wore wigs, but people such as bishops and judges were dressed in full-length wigs of the style worn by high court judges today. Thus they became known as big wigs.

Our present use of the phrase describes anybody who is a leading figure or a person of great importance. Some people talk and act as though they are somebody when they are nobody. But truly big people are those who think more about others than they do of themselves. Oddly enough, real VIPs are usually humble people, as the following stories show.

In December 1976 a national daily paper reported that one night an admiral in full dress uniform had been seen pushing his broken-down car in Trafalgar Square, London, in the pouring rain. At the driving wheel, and in the dry, sat his marine chauffeur! (I wonder whether Lord Nelson looked down from his lofty column with a mischievous smile at the unbelievable sight before his one eye!)

In 1963, about a fortnight after taking command of a Salvation Army corps in County Durham, I was told that I would be expected to pay a visit to a peer of the realm. 'When you find his lordship at home,' said my informant, 'you'll probably see him washing up at the sink by the kitchen window as you approach the back door.'

The thought of seeing such a distinguished person doing after-dinner chores was fascinating. It certainly cut across my childhood image of the 'favourites of fortune' in their palatial homes set in acres of beautiful grounds studded with majestic oak trees, and profusions of flowers of every species and hue.

I also visualised the Rolls Royce saloon tenderly polished by a devoted chauffeur. And to complete the mental picture I saw the servants going about their work in bee-like fashion, always eager to please their master and mistress.

Indeed, the lord I was about to meet seemed unique. One who gladly bent himself to do menial tasks despite the means, I presumed he had, to employ domestic staff. If only for this reason he would be an interesting person to visit.

The power of past mental images of the lordly was still strong with me, so it was with a degree of nervousness that I set out to make my acquaintance. Reaching the proximity of his home, and although expecting it to be a lowlier place than that I've described, I was directed to an astonishingly humble, terrace-type miner's cottage, where Lord (and Lady) Lawson of Beamish lived!

37

There he dwelt among some of the miners for whom he'd both toiled and fought, especially during the hungry days of the depression of the 1920s and 30s. It was his concern for their plight that had forged his links with The Salvation Army to whose work he gave practical support.

The coming of the Lord of lords in the form of a helpless baby called Jesus at Bethlehem, and being born in a stable at that, caused confusion in the minds of certain elite religious leaders of his day. Their spiritual pride couldn't accept that their Messiah would come in such an undignified manner. However, the truth stands forever that there, in that lowly place, God, in the person of Jesus Christ, became a human being.[1]

God, in Jesus, identified himself with us by sharing our life. He experienced feelings known to all human beings. He studied at school. He worked as a carpenter. He knew what it's like to be poor. He suffered bereavement. He endured all kinds of temptation. He suffered great pain. He performed lowly tasks which were far below the dignity of some of the big wigs of his day. This was especially so when he washed the feet of his uneducated, working-class disciples—for them an unforgettable lesson in humility. But this great act was a mere shadow of what he was about to do for all mankind by giving his life on the cross.

But that wasn't all he did for us, because he overcame death itself by rising from the grave. In Jesus we see the loving heart of the Father in Heaven made visible. Jesus is God's answer to the human heart cry: 'Does God care?' And by his death and glorious resurrection, his peace, joy and power are available to all humble enough to admit their need of him and who accept him as their Saviour and guide.

---

1 See John 1:1-14

15

They were caught napping

WE are told that the Saxon word *knaeppian* (meaning 'to doze') is the origin of our word 'nap'. A nap has been described as a brief period of sleep not taken in bed. Sometimes we have a nap as we travel, for instance, on a long-distance train or coach journey. Some people fall into a nap when they are bored with, say, a TV programme or a dry, lifeless sermon. Have you heard of the minister who fell asleep one Sunday afternoon while sitting in his study listening to a tape recording of his own sermon?

Some people's mid-afternoon nap is more like a middle-of-the-night deep sleep. Only an earthquake, it seems, would wake them. But when we talk about having a cat-nap, that's different. It means that, like a cat, although apparently asleep we can be instantly ready for action.

While stationed in Egypt on a Royal Air Force desert camp during the Second World War, I took my turn as sergeant in charge of the guard. It was a 24-hour tour of duty. As the guard commander, I was responsible to the duty officer, with whom I toured the sentry posts, for the guard's effectiveness. Any serviceman will tell you that a sentry never knows when a visit to test his alertness will take place. The obvious reason is to keep him constantly vigilant.

I vividly recall making our rounds of the sentry posts one particularly dark night during the early hours of a new day when the sentries' alertness would be difficult to maintain. As the RAF duty officer and I approached the position of a sentry on the camp's perimeter, an electric torch illuminating the ground for only a few feet ahead, a voice suddenly shouted from the darkness in front of us. 'Halt! Who goes there?' Obeying the command and replying, 'Friend', we then carefully advanced to be recognised. Soon our torch shone on the face of a West African soldier, his rifle and fixed bayonet pointing threateningly toward us, his face tense and his eyes fixed on ours. He was fully alert, despite the hour, and we were relieved. Had he been drowsy he might have pulled the trigger of his loaded rifle in a fit of panic. If marks had been awarded for being ready to meet a possible foe, he would have received 10 out of 10.

Let me tell you of another wartime experience, one for which *I wasn't* prepared. 'The king is coming!' shouted the driver in urgent tones as a police car pulled up at my side. I was the corporal in charge of a flight of RAF men destined for the North Africa campaign, but at the time on a route march along leafy lanes in Cheshire. Having received such unexpected and startling news, I was left to think what to do as the police car sped on its mission of 'preparing the way' for the king.

The incident reminded me of the dilemma of the grand old Duke of York who, halfway up the hill, didn't know whether to march his 10,000 men up to the top or down to the bottom! For a few fleeting moments I too was in a quandary with my 150 men! After all, wasn't it unreasonable of his majesty to 'drop in' on members of his air force without warning? I knew the drill for a planned, ceremonial parade on the barrack square, but in a country lane we were certainly unprepared for the coming of the king! There was only one thing to do. I told the men about the sovereign's imminent arrival and ordered them to march 'to attention' instead of 'at ease', the usual manner for route marches.

Within two minutes, a fleet of limousines, including the royal saloon bearing His Majesty King George VI, approached us. As the men marched on I stood to attention and saluted at the side of the road as the royal car passed by, on its way (we later learned) to a nearby military aircraft factory.

The Bible speaks about the return of Jesus, the King of kings. It's an event for which everybody should be ready by accepting him as Saviour and then living and working to receive his approval when he comes. Christians call this happening the second coming; his first coming was as a baby in Bethlehem. Warning us to be ready for his coming, Jesus told a story about 10 bridesmaids who had to wait a very long time before the bridegroom arrived. Five kept themselves prepared; the other five became weary of waiting. Let us read this part of the story from the Bible itself: 'The bridegroom was late in coming, so the girls began to nod and fall asleep'.[1]

When the bridegroom eventually came, at midnight, he caught them napping. Jesus ends his story with a stern warning: 'Be on your guard, then, because you do not know the day or the hour'.[2]

Are you spiritually ready for the coming of the King of kings? Don't be caught napping!

---

1 Matthew 25:5   2 Matthew 25:13

16

She took umbrage

THE Latin word 'umbra' means 'shade'. And the noun 'umbrella' comes from this root. Although those of us who live in rainy climates might think that the umbrella was invented to shelter us from showers, it was in fact brought into being to shade its user from the hot sun in tropical lands. And it has been around for many centuries. It wasn't until about 1760 that the umbrella was introduced in England as a protection from rain.

Who among us today could ever imagine that the harmless, indeed helpful, umbrella's arrival could cause a riot? But that is what happened! We often hear of stiff opposition to the introduction of cost-cutting, new methods and machines in industry, because they appear to threaten the livelihood of workers. Eventually the opponents have to give way and ultimately everybody recognises the universal benefits from such advances. This is no new phenomenon.

When the umbrella arrived in 18th-century England, the coachmen and sedan-chair men, whose covered-in carriages provided travellers with their only protection in wet weather, became incensed. They not only saw red, but thought their businesses would go into the red if their passengers became pedestrians carrying these newfangled brollies! Although we can't condone their rioting, we can sympathise with their anxious reasoning.

To take umbrage usually means, for example, that we feel resentment at being overshadowed or perhaps made to look small. For some people it's because somebody overtakes them and gains a position they felt they should have been given. Another way in which we might take umbrage is when we are worn down by the continuous, irritating actions of other people.

We've all heard of Sir Winston Churchill but few know about Jock, his cat. In 1974, Jock was still alive and well although he was said to be a bit crotchety at the grand old age of 12! During the spring and summer of that year 155,000 people visited the place where Jock lived because it happened to be Chartwell House, Kent, in England, the home of his late owner. Because Jock was the cat that Churchill stroked, many of those tourists stroked Jock so that on returning home they could boast of having stroked the cat that Churchill stroked! It isn't surprising to learn that Jock took umbrage, especially when, in the evening of life, a fellow likes to enjoy a bit more peace. We can understand his reaction when, having to endure those countless petty annoyances, he sometimes found his patience exhausted and gave vent to his pent up feelings with a sudden, hurtful, retaliatory stroke with a powerful front paw!

Sometimes umbrage is taken when younger folk tactlessly tell their elders what they should have done. Older people don't always take kindly to this. An amusing story comes from an eventide home run by The Salvation Army. A 97-year-old woman was obviously taking umbrage because a younger woman—a mere 91-year-old!—was telling her what she should do. Finally she angrily rounded on her 'junior' adviser with: 'Look here! I'm not taking advice from a bit of a girl like you'!

Occasionally some people feel overshadowed by people with greater knowledge or wisdom than their own. But there is no need to feel inferior. We all have something to offer to others. Strangely enough, some of the most learned people think they know so little. Lord Kelvin, the famous inventor of telegraphic and scientific instruments, was like that. When he was honoured with the Freedom of the City of Edinburgh he was asked to sign the visitors' book. Under the column headed 'Profession' he simply wrote 'Student'.

The Bible story of John the Baptist is a fascinating one. He blazed the trail for the coming of Jesus, the Messiah. Although he enjoyed outstanding success as a preacher, with hundreds becoming his followers, one day the tide turned and the people flocked to listen to Jesus instead. John was certainly being overshadowed by our Lord. But he didn't show jealousy. He didn't take umbrage. Earlier John confessed to the crowds that he wasn't good enough even to untie Christ's sandals. He certainly had the right attitude. Of course, John the Baptist had from the start of his ministry decided that it wasn't himself, but God, in Christ, who had to receive the glory for the change that would take place in the lives of those who accepted his message. And showing the ascendancy of Jesus, John said, 'He must become more important while I become less important.'[1]

Come to think of it, it's man's (and woman's!) inflated ideas of his own importance over his fellow men that causes so much trouble not only in the world at large but just where he lives. Only by inviting Jesus to

44

become the most important person in our lives can we hope unconsciously to display a humility like John's. And this would make our world a far happier place.

---

1 John 3:30

17
She saved her bacon

THE word 'bacon' originates from Old English *baec,* meaning back or body. When we say, 'She saved her bacon' we mean that she has escaped unhurt from a difficult or dangerous circumstance. It's right, of course, that we should do all we can to preserve body, mind and spirit (and, indeed, our reputation!) from harm. Self-preservation is a God-implanted instinct working powerfully within each of us. And don't we see it operating in animals and birds? We need only open the back door of a house to go into the garden and birds on the lawn immediately take flight to escape possible harm.

Sometimes people recklessly, and needlessly, face dangers and are fortunate to come out unscathed. Others unknowingly risk their lives and their 'bacon is saved' only by a prompt rescue operation. This is what happened to a middle-aged woman admitted to hospital after being found on the floor at home unable to get up. And while in hospital she had a heart attack and at one point her heart stopped beating.

The national newspaper reporting this incident added: 'Investigations showed the heart arrest to be due to the 4 lbs of liquorice sweets she was eating every week. The liquorice was also responsible for a muscle weakness which in turn was responsible for her having fallen on the floor and been unable to get up.'

You'll be glad (and perhaps relieved, if you are a liquorice allsorts lover!) to learn that, after doctors banned these sweets from her diet, the woman made a complete recovery. The *British Medical Journal* report on this strange case said that following three liquorice-less months all the laboratory tests carried out on the woman showed her body had returned to normal and she remained well. She had just saved her bacon! But thanks to the medical profession!

Come to think of it we owe a great debt of gratitude to researchers in various sciences who over many years have sacrificed time, money, health and, for some, even life itself to achieve great benefits for mankind. Advances in medical science, for example, which produced cures for diseases once regarded as incurable, are the results of sacrificial toil in laboratories, sometimes far into the night. Saving lives is a costly business. We often hear of brave people whose attempts to save the lives of others end in the loss of their own. I read of an unmarried man in a concentration camp who offered to take the place of a fellow prisoner condemned to death, because the man had a wife and children who needed him. That selfless, brave man was a Christian priest.

There was another man who sacrificed his life by taking my place—and yours!—so that we could escape the ultimate penalty of sin. That man was Jesus Christ. He was in fact God himself in human form, as the Bible so clearly tells us. It was because he loved each of us so much that he took our place on the cross so that we could be saved.

As he hung dying on the cross, people from three different classes joined forces to jeer at him. They shouted that if he was who he claimed to be, why didn't he save himself. Their rude remarks are recorded in the Bible: 'The Jewish leaders jeered at him: "He saved others; let him save himself if he is the Messiah whom God has chosen!" The soldiers also mocked him: they came up to him and offered him cheap wine, and said, "Save yourself if you are the king of the Jews!" . . . (And) . . . One of the criminals hanging there hurled insults at him: "Aren't you the Messiah? Save yourself and us!"'[1] But saving their own life isn't, and can't be, the first concern of life-savers, as I tried to show earlier.

In God's plan for our salvation, Jesus had to die so that we might live. And for what kind of life did he die? Let us hear from his own lips, words which give the answer. He said, 'I have come in order that you might have life—life in all its fullness'.[2]

He has, then, done his part. We must do ours by accepting, on his terms, the gift of salvation and the quality of life he came to give us.

---

1 Luke 23:35, 36, 39   2 John 10:10

18

She was a grass widow

THE expression 'a grass widow' was first used in British India to describe a woman temporarily separated from her husband during the hottest season of the year. It was to escape the oppressive heat of the plains that wives and their children went to the cool, high altitude of the hills. And it was there, in the nearer-to-temperate climate, that the grass grew, hence the description 'a grass widow'.

It was one thing to be a grass widow, although a frustrating and testing time if she was happily married. But it must be a devastating experience for a woman to be separated from her beloved husband by death.

Perhaps tribute should be paid to thousands of widows for their courage. Some of them face life without the comfort of grown-up children and the joy of grandchildren. Others are left with young children to bring up on a drastically-reduced income. It is not uncommon to hear people pay tribute to their mothers, widowed early in marriage, who worked and struggled to give their children a good start in life.

I like the hopeful spirit of a young 19th-century American widow. On her husband's tombstone she had inscribed, 'Sacred to the memory of James H. Random who died 6 August 1800. His widow who mourns as one who can be comforted, aged 24, and possessing every qualification for a good wife, lives at No 4 Church Street, in this village'! She certainly deserved and, I hope, found another good husband!

The courageous spirit which says 'life must go on' or more precisely in her case, 'business as usual', was shown by a French widow. On her husband's gravestone was written, 'Here lies Pierre Victor Fournier, inventor

49

of the Everlasting Lamp, which consumes only one centime's worth of oil in one hour. He was a good father, son and husband. His inconsolable widow continues his business in the Rue aux Trois. Goods sent to all parts of the city. Do not mistake the opposite shop for this.'! With such determination that her husband's business should prosper, and despite her great sorrow, she proved not only worthy of commercial success but, what is more important, that she had a brave heart.

We are told that women live longer than men. The presence of large numbers of elderly widows and relatively few widowers around us seems to verify this. That being the case it's obvious that many of these women not only live alone but are lonely.

Does God have a soft spot in his heart for widows? Perhaps it'll be comforting to them to learn that, although his love reaches to everybody, the Bible shows God has a special concern for widows. In it we find about 70 references to widows and widowhood. And to some people it might seem there is a hint of sex discrimination because the Bible doesn't mention the widower at all! But, of course, that idea is foreign to the nature of God's love.

Perhaps this apparent favouring of widows found in the Scriptures is to emphasise that women are, in God's sight, equal to men. In ancient times (and sadly, it's almost the same today) women in the East were regarded as only third-class citizens if not slaves. They existed chiefly to wait on men. But the Bible says, 'there is no difference . . . between men and women; you are all one in union with Christ Jesus'.[1]

Our Lord showed great respect for women and perhaps the fine qualities of character found in his mother gave him this. And did you know it is thought that Mary, his mother, became a widow before Jesus left home to begin his ministry? Our Lord, then, had first-hand experience of the sorrow and problems that confront widows and understands how hard life can be for many of them.

The Bible contains interesting stories of women bereft

of their husbands. One of the greatest is that of Naomi and her daughter-in-law Ruth, both of whom became widows. If you want a moving story of two women whose faith in God continued to shine, despite the bitter experience of widowhood, and how God rewarded them, this is one to read. You can find it in the Old Testament. And it's also a love story with a happy ending!

Boaz, the man who was later to become Ruth's second husband, said to her, 'May the Lord reward you for what you have done. May you have a full reward from the Lord God of Israel, to whom you have come for protection!' Ruth answered, 'You are very kind to me, sir. You have made me feel better by speaking gently to me, even though I am not the equal of one of your servants'.[2]

When her mother-in-law, Naomi, heard of Boaz's kind words, she exclaimed, 'May the Lord bless Boaz!' And she said to Ruth, 'The Lord always keeps his promises to the living and the dead'. And she continued, 'That man is a close relative of ours, one of those responsible for taking care of us.'[3]

God uses many kinds of situations to bring his people closer to himself, and others to accept his loving rule over their lives for the first time. In Ruth's case God used her sorrow to draw her to himself. That highlight experience happened when she said to Naomi, who served the living God, 'Your God will be my God'.[4]

From that moment her heart was open to receive the blessings and protection God had for her. It's only after we decide for God, as revealed in Jesus Christ, that we can fully experience all the good things he wants to give us, whether widows, widowers or whoever we are.

---

1 Galatians 3:28   2 Ruth 2:12, 13
3 Ruth 2:20   4 Ruth 1:16*b*

19
They've settled a bargain

'IT'S settled! It's a deal! Let's shake hands!' we exclaim. It's a happy moment. Sometimes it's the beginning of a renewed friendship.

Do you know that a 'settle' is a wooden bench with a high back and arms? We are told that a settle was the place on which quarrels or bargainings were settled. This appears to be the reason why a satisfactory agreement reached on a settle became known as a matter that had been settled. It is similar to saying, for example, that we cycled, to indicate that we arrived on a cycle.

The word 'settle', of course, has had other meanings added. But some of them also relate to achieving a happy result—peace, contentment. For instance, we might say, 'They have settled in Canada' meaning they have happily adjusted to life in their new land. And if the weatherman forecasts settled weather, that is also pleasing, especially if we are on holiday!

To return to bargains, though, let me tell you a true story from my own life. It was on a mild, sunny Saturday in mid-autumn 1978 that it happened. Having enjoyed our in-the-car picnic lunch on a cliff top overlooking the sea, my wife suggested we should tour the shops. (And every husband knows how exciting that is!)

The trouble is, some wives can't be content looking for bargains in ordinary shops. They have an eye for posters announcing, by implication at least, *real* bargains. So on the day mentioned, I found myself reluctantly giving permission to my wife to enter ('just for a few minutes' she promised) an empty shop being used for a jumble sale.

Permission received, she flew *inside* and left me *outside*. After two minutes, which seemed like two hours, I peered through the shop window hoping to signal that her time was nearly up. But it was no good. She was too busy examining a captivating collection of knick-knacks.

About eight hours later—eight minutes in actual time!—she emerged in triumph. 'Look,' she exclaimed, 'I've bought this—only 10p.' I looked, and I could tell—and she could see—that my face showed not even a flicker of enthusiasm. But perhaps I could be forgiven, because, as I looked at the article in her hand, I had to ask myself whether I was dreaming. The answer was an immediate and firm *no*! Then I asked myself, 'Aren't we already married? Then what's my wife doing with this article—a bride's veil?'

Many years had passed since she promised: 'I will', and said so happily in her Salvation Army uniform. Now, I wondered, was this veil a veiled hint that she had, after all, longed for a white wedding? And was she hoping for a public renewal of our marriage vows on our next wedding anniversary—this time in white?

But no! The solution to the puzzle soon came to light. And I saw that she was the one who was dreaming. She had a vision of a doll dressed in beautiful clothes made from this veil—and made by grandma! 'Won't it bring happiness to a little grand-daughter!' A little grand-daughter, did she say?

Then I remembered she *is* a grandma! And I knew that she would soon reach her first anniversary, as a grandma, that is. But I thought it was the arrival of a grand*son* that promoted her to that élite company of ladies, and I was sure she had no reason to believe another grandchild was expected.

Nevertheless, I realised my wife is a woman of vision. She saw what that veil could become in *her* hands. After all, isn't it true that we enjoy many great benefits and pleasures brought about by people who began with a vision? It was said of Michelangelo, the sculptor, that in every block of granite he saw an angel. And his beautiful works have given enjoyment to thousands.

There is another person who had a vision, the greatest-ever vision for man's good. That person is God our heavenly Father. His vision of what man could become was realised when he sent his Son Jesus Christ to be our Saviour. In his life and teaching Jesus showed us how a human being could portray the beauty of character found in God his Father. And if we placed ourselves in *his* hands, he would reproduce his nature in us. We should become like him.[1]

To have his likeness, our Lord said we should begin by seeking a personal settlement in our relationship with God. The Bible speaks about a mercy seat. Somebody has described it as the throne of God. It was there, at the mercy seat, that, before Christ came, the high priest had to plead with God for mercy and pardon for his sinning people.

Our personal mercy seat could be our bedside, or the pew or communion rail in a church. It might be the bench in a Salvation Army hall which is actually called a mercy seat. Whether it is a physical thing, such as those mentioned, isn't really important, although public confession has proved helpful to most people. The spiritual mercy seat, the essential one, is found in our souls. Those who have knelt at the mercy seat and settled things with God, through repentance and faith in Christ, speak of a deep peace within. A Salvation Army song writer put it like this: 'My soul has found a resting place, And I am now, through heavenly grace, At peace with God. . . .'

Of course, we don't bargain with God, but, besides his peace and presence, he does promise other good things to those who come to terms with his will for them. And they are far more exciting than the best of this world's so-called bargains!

---

1 See 2 Peter 1:1-8

20

It's been earmarked for you

THE word 'earmarked' originally indicated the marking of cattle and sheep with their owner's identification mark on one of the ears. Today we normally use it to denote something that has been set aside for a special purpose or a particular person. Earmarking has even been performed on human beings. This goes back to at least the centuries immediately before Christ and it too was to identify their owner. Under the law of Moses, a Hebrew slave, who had probably been compelled by his family's financial need to give himself to servitude, could exercise his right to freedom after six years' compulsory service. He could also elect to stay as a servant, but one condition was that he had to express his love for his master. After approval to remain in service was given, a ceremony took place at a place used for worship. During the proceedings the master pierced his servant's ear as he stood against a door, or door post, and this was witnessed by judicial officials. Indeed, from that moment he became a marked man! He had been earmarked, willingly and happily, for what might become a life-time of service as a slave in his master's household.

Thinking of owners' identification marks, one that springs to mind is that of our finger prints, which are different from those of anybody else. That is why the careful burglar or criminal wears gloves! He knows his finger prints are his and nobody else's! They identify *him* as the owner.

Although many millions of people populate the world, God has made each of us different. Each of us is unique. There may be likenesses but no one is exactly like anybody else. Have you ever noticed that a person whose mannerisms are familiar to us can be identified even at a distance, for instance, by the very way in which he or she walks?

A friend of mine was to be measured for a new Salvation Army uniform. Before setting out from home his wife advised him, 'Tell them that your shoulders are twisted, your arms are too long for your body, your legs are out of proportion and you are pigeon-toed!' Having been married to him for about 40 years, his wife should know about his unique figure! But she still loves him just as he is!

It is the fact that everybody is different that makes people so interesting. One of the things that we might say about a robot, described as an 'apparently human automaton . . . but impersonal machine', is that its sameness in mechanical movement (and monotone voice, in some cases) is positively boring. It lacks the colour, warmth and uniqueness of a human being.

Perhaps it goes without saying that since God has made each of us different then he has a unique plan for each of our lives. God's general command, communicated through the Bible and culminating in the teaching of Jesus, is that his love must rule our hearts. But he has also earmarked a particular service for each of us through which his love can reach others.

Jesus invited the people to take upon themselves his yoke. This was a symbol of his teaching, but we may also regard it as a yoke personally fashioned by him to fit our unique personality. Let us remember that before he began his ministry, Jesus worked as a carpenter in Nazareth, his home town. Probably, he made hundreds of wooden yokes during those years. I can imagine that because they were made by Jesus, each one of them was perfect in design and workmanship. Just as my friend's Salvation Army uniform would, hopefully, be tailored to fit his unique figure, so each yoke created by Jesus would perfectly fit only the oxen for which he made it.

It is a marvellous truth that, although those animals

weren't aware of it, they went about their work wearing yokes made by Jesus of Nazareth, son of Joseph and the Son of God. They wouldn't understand why, but his yokes would be supremely comfortable, even soothing, on their necks. May I suggest that perhaps Jesus, remembering how blessed those oxen were, had this thought in mind when he said to the people listening to his teaching, 'Come to me, all of you who are tired from carrying heavy loads, and I will give you rest. Take my yoke and put it on you, and learn from me, because I am gentle and humble in spirit; and you will find rest. For the yoke I will give you is easy, and the load I will put on you is light.'[1]

Let us think again about the Hebrew slave who gladly elected to continue in his master's service. Obviously he found him to be fair, kind and had shown concern for his family's welfare during six years' compulsory service. Perhaps we can even presume the slave was even proud of the earmark because he belonged to a good master.

Those who, of their own free will, accept the yoke made and offered by Jesus become identified with him by their Christlike living. And their very countenance shows they are possessed by Christ's peace and joy. Indeed, they are marked out as people who belong to and gladly serve their Lord and Master.

---

1 Matthew 11:28-30

21
He's often
in the limelight

THIS saying is used to describe people frequently in the full glare of public attention; for example, certain members of the British royal family. They in particular seem unable to go anywhere in the world without being pursued by an army of journalists, photographers and TV cameras.

Where did this saying originate? It came from the theatre. Before the days of gas and electric lighting, the stage was illuminated by light produced from lime. The limelight was created by a blow-pipe flame directed against a block of pure, compressed quicklime. Actors of those times were literally in the limelight!

Many internationally known people tire of being continually in the public eye. Some seek to disguise themselves and their identity as they travel the world by wearing dark glasses and checking-in at airports and hotels under assumed names. They long to be less noticed because they are over-noticed. Nevertheless, in each human being is an instinctive need to be noticed. Provided it's because of a worthy achievement most of us enjoy some limelight! This hunger for recognition is more readily seen in a child. For instance, a young boy who proudly shows an adult his painting hopes for commendation. If he receives it his confidence grows and it helps him to develop not only his talents, but into a balanced person.

In 1951, when I was in charge of the Salvation Army corps in Sandwich, Kent, one of the Cinque Ports, the then Lord Warden of these ports visited the town. He was Sir Winston Churchill. For this occasion, my wife and I felt privileged to be invited to join others in forming a guard of honour outside the guild-hall. I had heard this great statesman's famous wartime speeches on the radio which brought hope to millions both in the free world and those under Nazi domination. On this sunny June morning I set out with the hope of not only seeing my wartime hero, but actually shaking hands with him. And I don't think I was the only one with that hope!

When Churchill's limousine pulled up, he stepped out, walked between the two rows of personally-invited people and, without glancing either to the left or right, he disappeared into the ancient building. He hadn't appeared to notice any other member of the guard of honour, let alone me. We weren't to be in the limelight that day after all!

In contrast, there is the heart-warming story about Queen Elizabeth the Queen Mother's visit in April 1983 to Brixton, a part of south London with a high percentage of West Indians. A national daily paper said, 'She made the front line district of Railton Road, flashpoint of past riots, her own'. More than 1,000 people of different colours waiting in the pouring rain were astonished to find that when the Queen Mother's car drew up, she headed straight for them rather than the waiting dignitaries and the shelter of the senior citizen's centre she had come to open.

One West Indian woman, who had waited two hours in the rain, called out, 'She is beautiful! Just beautiful!' And she was delighted when the 82-year-old Queen Mother paused to shake her hand. For 10 minutes the royal visitor braved the elements without an umbrella to talk to the crowds who had gathered to cheer her. Another West Indian woman said, 'She shook my hand —and now everyone is telling me not to wash it. She is a wonderful person. This is a great day for everyone who lives here'. She had not only noticed them but talked with and shaken hands with them. Indeed, it was an unforgettable day when these ordinary people were in the limelight because of the Queen Mother's personal interest!

But what about those who hunger for recognition but never seem to catch the eye of anybody, let alone a queen? Maybe only a few of us regard some people as worth noticing, but the Bible says that God always has his loving eyes on everybody. For example, one day when Jesus was talking to his disciples he told them that his heavenly Father knew each of them intimately and cared about them personally. This is how he put it: 'For only a penny you can buy two sparrows, yet not one sparrow falls to the ground without your Father's consent. As for you, even the hairs of your head have all been counted. So do not be afraid; you are worth much more than many sparrows!'[1]

Obviously, Jesus had a great sense of humour and I can imagine a twinkle in his eye when he told them God had counted the hairs on each of their heads. It was true, but telling it in this manner he probably made them laugh. That would please him because there's plenty of room for good, clean fun in our Lord's way of life. But he was driving home the great lesson that their heavenly Father was closely and lovingly watching and caring for them. And that truth applies to us today, too!

We may rest assured that each of us, without exception, is in God's limelight while we are on life's stage, especially when our leading role in life is to act according to the spirit of the script he has written for us in the Bible. And so, with his presence and help, perform our part on this earthly stage in the way which pleases him!

---

1 Matthew 10:29-31

22
Let me kiss the place and make it better

PROBABLY every English-speaking mother uses this saying to comfort her young child when he hurts himself. The phrase has a surprising background. It's linked with the sorcerer, a person described as one who works magic for evil purposes. To cure somebody bitten by an adder he would pretend merely to kiss the bite. In fact he simply sucked out the snake's poison! But the common people were led to believe the sorcerer had performed a miracle by his kiss and we can imagine the awe with which they viewed him!

There is no doubt, of course, that a mother's kiss on the hurt place works wonders! The child quickly forgets his minor injury as happily he runs off to play again knowing that mother had fully sympathised with him.

The idea of a kiss bringing healing and restoring joy to the life of a small child reminds us that this sign of mutual affection between human beings does bring an extra degree of happiness to their lives. It makes them feel they are really loved by the other person and that in itself is a healing balm to mind and spirit.

Some people might be surprised to learn that in the Bible there are about 40 references to kissing. The kiss, of course, is a common salutation in the East. When mentioned in the Scriptures it is usually to record its use as a sign of love between relatives, and an expression of Christian love between members of the Early Church.

With a few exceptions, such as Judas's kiss of betrayal of our Lord, the kiss is given with pure motives. It is in times of distress, as with the occasion when a child hurts himself, that a kiss makes many people feel better. They find the pangs of their sorrow or other trouble are relieved by this compassionate act shown by close relatives and friends.

As I was walking through the grounds of a hospital to visit a patient, a window cleaning contractor's van passed me and on the back I read, 'Your panes give us pleasure'. Fortunately, I recognised the panes referred to were plates of glass fitted into window frames, so immediately I got the clever publicity message! If I hadn't known the difference in spelling of the two same-sounding words, I might angrily have thought the van's owners took a distasteful delight in watching people in pain. And because the vehicle was in hospital grounds, my disgust would have deepened. Unfortunately, some folk do have a reputation for revelling in other people's troubles, and others of their kind enjoy making hurtful comments. This evil, it seems, has been around for centuries. The Bible shows it has when it says, 'Some people like to make cutting remarks'. But then it advises, 'But the words of the wise soothe and heal'.[1]

Because our fellow human beings are seemingly often troubled and anxious (and none of us escapes these unwelcome experiences) we should spend far more time supporting each other with words of comfort and encouragement, of hope and optimism. And remember there is one person—Jesus Christ—whose 'wonderful words of life' have a far more beneficial effect upon us than any merely human words—or kiss, for that matter—could have. In fact, his words have the power to heal the whole of our personality—body, mind and spirit!

---

1 Proverbs 12:18, *LB*

23
He let himself go to pot

THIS saying came into our language at some time following the first discovery that stolen gold and silver articles were being put into a melting pot so that their identity would be completely lost and therefore untraceable.

Our use of the phrase is chiefly to describe someone who, because of some devastating experience in family or business life, has lost the will to carry on and turns in on himself as he ceases to show any interest in the world about him. Some of these sad people become recluses and seemingly all of them neglect their appearance, home and everything else that once received regular care and attention. Their former identity as smart, disciplined and alert people can no longer be seen. They have gone to pot.

People who remember the Second World War might recall the 1940 appeal to Britain's housewives to donate aluminium pots and pans because of the acute shortage of this metal, needed in the production of military aircraft. Because those pans would also be thrown into melting pots they too would lose their identity. But losing themselves as pans they would become part of the fight to save the nation from enslavement by a ruthless dictator.

Perhaps we can see from this illustration that in one sense 'going to pot' can lead to a new and even more useful kind of life. When we come to think of it, the way of life offered to us by Jesus Christ involves losing our identity as selfish people and being changed into people whose first aim is to live for God and others. This doesn't mean, of course, that we have to neglect ourselves. But remarkable transformations have taken place in the lives of people who have committed themselves to Christ's purpose for them. Although they are still recognised by their physical features, their character and spirit have changed for the good. Whereas, for example, they lied their way through life they are now truthful; once they were mean, now they are generous; formerly they were spiteful in their remarks, perhaps to their nearest and dearest, now they are gentle and gracious in what they say.

Their relatives and acquaintances can't identify these people as being the same in character and attitude. Thankfully, they have lost their former ugly selves and become the kind of folk we like to be with.

This loss of the old, selfish life and finding new life is, then, what our Lord meant when he said, 'If anyone wants to come with me, he must forget self, carry his cross, and follow me. For whoever wants to save his own life will lose it; but whoever loses his life for my sake will find it.'[1]

To remain anonymous if we had, for instance, created something that somebody else takes and handles with such outstanding skill so that he receives worldwide praise, would be a hard thing to do. It takes a big-hearted and truly humble person to do that. A Mr Bert Smith was of that rare kind of human being.

The name Yehudi Menuhin is universally known as that of a famous violinist. But whoever has heard of Bert Smith the man who, before he died in 1976, was Menuhin's violin maker? If we go to St Andrew's Church, Coniston, in England's lakeland we should see a plaque to his memory. It was said of him that he produced exquisite violins with tools made by himself and that his work was 'out of this world'. The famous player of some of those beautiful violins has been applauded and received standing ovations around the world, but few, if any, in his audiences will have made even a passing enquiry about who made Yehudi's violins.

Even a great violinist wouldn't be able to bring beautiful sounds from a badly-made violin but only from a superbly-created instrument such as Bert Smith produced. Nevertheless, Bert was content to remain anonymous and let his friend, Yehudi Menuhin, receive acclamation for the beauty of tone produced by his masterly touch but equally because he performed on an exquisite violin. Doubtless that famous player would be the first to recognise the indispensable part played by Bert Smith.

A man called John the Baptist, a contemporary of Jesus, wasn't only a forthright preacher but a forerunner of our Lord. He paved the way for Jesus as we can learn from words he spoke. John said, 'I am the voice of someone shouting in the desert: Make a straight path for the Lord to travel!' Then he declared: 'Among you stands the one you do not know. He is coming after me, but I am not good enough even to untie his sandals'.[2] And some time later, again speaking about Jesus, he said, 'He must become more important while I become less important'.[3]

This was another way of saying that our Lord must have more of the limelight. John, despite his great success in attracting and holding the crowds as a preacher, withdrew into the shadows. The great apostle Paul too spoke of the pre-eminence of Jesus when he affirmed, 'The life I now live is not my life, but the life which Christ lives in me'.[4]

Both of these great men gladly surrendered claims to self-recognition so that Jesus should receive the praise, honour and glory due only to him. And that, in part, is how they found eternal life!

---

1 Matthew 16:24, 25   2 John 1:23, 26, 27
3 John 3:30   4 Galatians 2:20, *NEB*

24
I was roped in to help

THIS saying has its origin in the cattle ranches of America. When an animal was brought in by lasso it was in fact roped in, the lasso, of course, being a long rope with a running noose. Our everyday use of the phrase usually means we have persuaded or cajoled somebody to help us with a task.

In his newsletter, a Salvation Army corps officer advertised a jumble sale to be held on a certain Saturday. He was obviously not only anxious to gather together an adequate collection of saleable items, but to get help from husbands among his flock. So in his appeal he included an unwittingly humorous reference to them. This is what he wrote: 'This is a chance to get rid of anything that is not worth keeping, but is too good to throw away. Wives are especially asked to bring their husbands!' You see what I mean?

This business of being helpful to others can be interesting to observe. There are some people whose help would come only if they were pushed into action like a hand-operated lawn-mower. (Many years ago I saw an old lawn-mower with the brand name, *Willing Worker*. I couldn't help saying to it, 'Yes, but you need pushing before you'll work!') Perhaps people who need pushing before they help others hold too narrow an interpretation of the saying that God helps those who help themselves. It certainly seems to be true that the only people they help is themselves. On the other hand there are people whose well-meaning help is soon found to be unhelpful. For instance, we might say of one of them, 'He meant well, but he made such a poor job of the painting'.

There are also folk whose help begins well and continues for a while, then they become weary in well doing, their enthusiasm fades and so does their help. When my eldest son was just over two years old, and my wife and I were packing our personal belongings before moving to take up another appointment as Salvation Army officers, he ran to help me transfer our books from the bookshelves to the room in which they were to be packed. At first, carrying about two or three at a time, he brought them to the spot where I needed them, near a tea chest. Then he began to deposit his small load a foot away from that precise point. The next pile was placed yet a farther foot from the previous one and this pattern was copied until there was a wavy line of books curling its way from the tea chest, across the room, through the open doorway, down the corridor and into the room containing the fast-emptying shelves! The spirit was willing but little legs and feet were becoming weary.

When relatives or friends are coming to stay with us do we ask family members to help us with the preparations? Or do we simply say the visitors will be welcome but they'll have to take us as they find us? Usually people do go out of their way in preparing to provide the best possible hospitality for guests, and generally it involves a lot of extra work for the woman of the home. It's not surprising if she becomes overtired and grumbles if others in the home don't help. There's a true story in the Bible about a woman like that. She was a follower of Jesus and her name was Martha. It was in her home in Bethany, where she lived with her sister Mary, that our Lord knew he could rest, relax and enjoy a meal. It was one of his favourite havens. In fact, it seems that Martha's home was held as 'open house' to anybody.

Let us read the account of what happened one day: 'As Jesus and his disciples went on their way, he came to a village where a woman named Martha welcomed him in her home. She had a sister named Mary, who sat down at the feet of the Lord and listened to his teaching. Martha was so upset over all the work she had to do, so she came and said, "Lord, don't you care that my sister has left me to do all the work by myself? Tell her to come and help me!" The Lord answered her, "Martha, Martha! You are worried and troubled over so many things, but just one is needed. Mary has chosen the right thing, and it will not be taken away from her".'[1]

The Lord's reply seems to confirm Martha was right: he didn't care about her need for Mary's help. But we may be sure he was never in favour of people standing idly by when others urgently needed assistance. Although it isn't recorded in the Bible, probably Jesus did tell Mary to go and help Martha. There is ample evidence to show our Lord himself was deeply concerned about giving practical help to ease the burdens of everyday life—for instance, he fed the hungry, healed the sick, and on one occasion he even cooked a meal for his tired disciples.[2] (It is worth remembering that Jesus feels just as much at home in a kitchen as in a cathedral).

Although he'd be the first to praise Martha's hard-working character, our Lord recognised she tended to become over-anxious about earthly matters and neglected to listen to what he had to say. But wiser people, like Mary, hunger for his words. They are words about divine forgiveness, love, joy; about life—eternal life. They are about the help everyone needs most of all. And it's the kind of help that only Jesus can offer to the world, as Charles Wesley clearly affirms in one of his hymns:

> *Jesus, transporting sound,*
> *The joy of earth and heaven;*
> *No other help is found,*
> *No other name is given*
> *By which we can salvation have;*
> *But Jesus came the world to save.*

---

1 Luke 10:38-42   2 See John 21:9-13

25

He had a busman's holiday

ON the face of it, this is an odd way to describe a holiday. Obviously, we can use this saying only if we know its meaning, so from what source did it come? Let us trace its origin by going back to the days of horse-drawn buses, which were, for example, an everyday sight on London's streets. We are told that some drivers of these vehicles became so attached to their horses that they spent their free days on the buses to ensure they were properly treated by drivers on duty. Because spending their free time in this way was doing almost the same thing as when at work, the habit became known as a busman's holiday. Our use of the saying echoes this when, for instance, we tell about a motor mechanic who spent his holidays repairing his own car. Or a typist who gave up her holidays to type, say, for a charity as an unpaid worker.

We know, of course, there are some people whose work, so they tell us, is their hobby. They don't need or want a holiday. If their families insist that they accompany them on holiday, they are miserable until once again they return to work. But such people are only a tiny minority.

And what about those folks whose work at times is of such importance and urgency that, temporarily, it prevents their departure for a break of even a few days. Some politicians holding top government posts occasionally find themselves in this situation. For example, during the Falklands crisis in the spring of 1982, the US Secretary of State, Alexander Haig, had the unenviable task of seeking to prevent war. It included shuttling between the USA and Great Britain and flying to and from Argentina many times. The travelling itself was exhausting and this was coupled with long, tense sessions in tough negotiations. When he completed his exacting mission, he said, 'I've been suffering from such jet lag recently that when I finished the Falklands shuttle I got off the plane, shook my wife's hand and kissed Casper Weinberger, the US Defence Secretary!' Well, at least his wife would certainly recognise he needed a holiday!

I suppose it would be true to say that having a busman's holiday, although the purpose of the original busman's holiday was commendable, is unwise since we all need a change from the everyday tasks which demand our energies of mind, hand and spirit. The word 'recreation' is linked in our thinking with enjoyable pursuits in our free time. But how many of us stop to think of the meaning of this word? It is simply 're-creation'—that is, renewal of our powers of body, mind and spirit. The re-creating process takes place as we rest and alternate this with doing things that are pleasure-giving and different from daily duties.

Jesus himself, being truly man as well as truly God (a basic belief held by Christians) recognised the need to rest and recuperate. His human body experienced hunger, thirst and weariness. His humanity is clearly observed in many of the stories about him in the Bible. A classic one reads, 'Jesus, tired out by the journey, sat down by the well. It was about noon. A Samaritan woman came to draw some water, and Jesus said to her, "Give me a drink of water".'[1] Immediately after this the Bible writer puts in, as an aside, the fact that his disciples had gone into town to buy food. So here we find our Lord tired, thirsty and hungry. He was, indeed, truly man!

Because he had, in part, come to earth to share the common lot of man, our Lord spent himself in service to them. He found he couldn't turn away the needy multitudes, although his human frame became weary and at times he longed for solitude. The wonderful thing was, having Jesus around was the greatest heart-warming experience ordinary people had ever had. What he said captivated them. Unlike those of the religious leaders of his day, his words were spoken with love and divine authority. And then for them to witness his healing of the sick was a 'must'. On one occasion, the Bible says (and it was typical of what happened almost every day), 'There were so many people coming and going that Jesus and his disciples didn't even have time to eat. So he said to them, "Let us go off by ourselves to some place where we will be alone and you can rest for a while". So they started out in a boat by themselves for a lonely place'.[2]

But the story goes on to tell us that the people followed them. The disciples' hoped-for place of rest became merely another place for Jesus to spend himself teaching and healing. Despite their Lord's plan to escape the demanding crowd for a much-needed rest, they were, for the time being, compelled to have a busman's holiday.

Perhaps when we go on our holidays we should spare a thought and offer a prayer for those whose home circumstances compel them to continue serving, for example, a chronically sick husband, parent or child. Maybe if we don't or can't take them a small gift from our holiday town when we return home, we could at least send them a picture postcard saying we remember them. It would certainly re-assure them of our love and concern.

---

1 John 4:6*b*, 7   2 Mark 6:31, 32

73

26
She served us Adam's ale

CALLING water Adam's ale is obviously an unconscious reminder that Adam, the first human being, had nothing but water to quench his thirst. During the summer of 1983 an oft-repeated news item told of a growing number of tourists who had become ill with typhoid after staying at a certain hotel on the Greek Island of Kos. At first it was thought that the water was contaminated.

Do you know that because of this very possibility Queen Elizabeth II carries bottles of Malvern spring water when she tours abroad? Pure drinking water is so easily obtained in lands such as Great Britain that it is taken for granted and almost despised. Yet if the world's water supplies became polluted and there was no means of purification we would all die within a short time. You see, we are told that we can live for about 60 days without food, but only a few days without water.

Let us imagine a situation in which we were guests in a friend's home and our hostess acted as though it was the normal social custom to serve water instead of, say, the more acceptable cup of tea or coffee, although on all previous visits we had received these drinks. I think it would be an unforgettable occasion. We might find it hard to resist the temptation to tell other friends about what happened. Although not wanting to appear ungrateful to our hostess, we might say something like this: 'We couldn't believe our eyes when Margaret, with the air of the perfect hostess, brought in a beautiful tray bearing a cut glass jug of sparkling water and four tumblers to match and, with her usual charm, poured out our drinks and handed them to us'. I imagine most of us would look with dismay at the sight before our eyes, and feel disappointed because our drink was water instead of a good-old cup of tea!

Our imaginary friend surprised us not only by serving water but also by offering no explanation and showing no embarrassment because she wasn't providing the usual beverages. Yet if we were dying of thirst in a desert, when help arrived our immediate and desperate plea would be for water. Can you think of yourself saying to the person who found you in that plight, 'O wonderful! I'm so glad you came. I wonder whether you'd make me a nice cup of coffee? Nescafé is my favourite brand. And make it with milk, please. Oh, and don't forget the sugar. Four teaspoonsful'.

Of course, that is an absurd idea. A particular choice of drink wouldn't even be thought of let alone requested. If you were in that dilemma you would rejoice because somebody had at last reached you with nothing more appetising than Adam's ale. You'd be keenly aware that pure water would mean continuing life for you since it has within it some of the ingredients vital to creating and sustaining life.

When the London Marathon was held in April 1983, the participants were offered cups of water at one-mile intervals along the 26-mile route. A commentator said that it was important to drink water long before the runners became thirsty, otherwise they would suffer from dehydration later in the race. And isn't it significant that, as scientists tell us, water makes up 60 per cent of our body weight?

Knowing better than anybody else that man is so dependent on water—and in the land in which he spoke about it its scarcity was a continual source of anxiety to everybody—Jesus pointedly referred to water to illustrate or describe the quality and everlasting nature of the life he offers mankind. Just as nobody would enjoy water for their 'elevenses' because it is tasteless, only relatively few people have made the great discovery that the seemingly unappetising water Jesus offers does in fact hold the secret of a deeply satisfying life which is eternal. No wonder Jesus said to a woman drawing water from a well, 'Whoever drinks this water will be thirsty again, but whoever drinks the water that I will give him will never be thirsty again. The water that I will give him will become in him a spring which will provide him with life-giving water and give him eternal life'.[1]

Like the man dying of thirst in a desert who knows his physical life will be saved only by the arrival of a rescuer with water, Adam's ale, it will be when we recognise that our soul's thirst can be quenched only by the spiritual water offered by Jesus, that we shall plead with the hymn-writer:

> *Thee let me drink and thirst no more*
> *For drops of finite happiness;*
> *Spring up, O Well, in heavenly power,*
> *In streams of pure perennial peace,*
> *In joy that none can take away,*
> *In life which shall for ever stay.*

---

1 John 4. 13, 14

John 1 - 4. 13 + 14